Jaguars

by Rachel Lynette

Consultant:
Dr. Mark C. Andersen
Department of Fish, Wildlife and Conservation Ecology
New Mexico State University

BEARPORT
PUBLISHING

New York, New York

Credits

Cover and Title, © D. Davids/WireImage/Getty Images; 4–5, © Gerard Lacz/Animals Animals; 6, © Red Line Editorial; 6–7, 23 (top), © Corbis/SuperStock; 8–9, 22 (bottom), © oriontrail/Shutterstock Images; 9, © Red Line Editorial; 10, 23 (middle), © NHPA/SuperStock; 10–11, © Minden Pictures/SuperStock; 12–13, 22 (middle), © Gerard Lacz Images/SuperStock; 14, © Gerard Lacz Images/SuperStock; 15, © Ryan M. Bolton/Shutterstock Images; 16, 22 (top), © E. Sweet/Shutterstock Images; 16–17, © Gerard Lacz Images/age fotostock/SuperStock; 18–19, © Cusp/SuperStock; 19, © Nick Garbutt/naturepl.com; 20–21, © Matt Hart/Shutterstock Images.

Publisher: Kenn Goin
Editor: Joy Bean
Creative Director: Spencer Brinker
Photo Researcher: Arnold Ringstad
Design: Emily Love

Library of Congress Cataloging-in-Publication Data in process at time of publication (2013)
Library of Congress Control Number: 2012039858
ISBN-13: 978-1-61772-755-9 (library binding)

For more information, write to Bearport Publishing Company, Inc., 45 West 21st Street, Suite 3B, New York, New York 10010. Printed in the United States of America.

10 9 8 7 6 5 4 3 2 1

Contents

Meet a jaguar cub

A mother jaguar lies down with her **cubs**.

They are resting in a grassy field near a river.

cubs

The cubs stays close to their mother to keep safe.

The mother will attack any enemies that come near.

mother jaguar

What is a jaguar?

Jaguars are large cats.

An adult jaguar can weigh up to 250 pounds (113 kg).

Most have tan fur with black spots, but some have dark fur and black spots.

Adult jaguar size

Jaguars have strong muscles and are skilled hunters.

They are built to **pounce** on their **prey**.

spots

adult jaguar

Where do jaguars live?

Jaguars mainly live in Central and South America.

Most of them live in **rain forests**.

Jaguars mothers make their **dens** in small caves.

Dens are safe places for baby jaguars to rest and hide from danger.

□ **Where jaguars live**

North America

Atlantic Ocean

Central America

South America

Pacific Ocean

N
W · E
S

jaguar den

9

Going for a swim

Jaguars often make their dens near water.

There, they can catch the fish they like to eat.

fish

They can also go for a nice swim when the weather is hot.

Unlike most other kinds of cats, jaguars are good swimmers.

cub swimming

Newborn cubs

A mother jaguar gives birth in her den.

She has from one to four babies at a time.

The newborn cubs are born with their eyes closed.

However, when they are eight days old, their eyes open.

A cub weighs just two pounds (0.9 kg) when it is born.

a mother jaguar
and her cub

Growing up

The cubs drink their mother's milk for five to six months.

When they are about two weeks old, they also begin to eat meat.

cub drinking milk

The milk and meat help them grow big and strong quickly.

They will need strength to fight off enemies, such as large snakes called anacondas.

Until they can defend themselves, however, their mother will protect them.

anaconda

Strong jaws

Jaguars are meat eaters.

They eat many kinds of animals, including fish, turtles, and **capybaras**.

With their powerful jaws and sharp teeth, adult jaguars can bite through a turtle's shell.

capybara

powerful
jaw

17

Learning to hunt

Jaguar cubs go on hunts with their mother when they are about six months old.

jaguar ready to pounce

They learn how to hunt by watching her.

They see her hide in trees or on riverbanks and wait for prey to pass by.

They watch as she pounces on the prey and kills it.

Then, mom and the cubs eat.

prey

Leaving the den

Jaguar cubs stay with their mother for about two years.

Once they leave, the grown-up male cubs live alone the rest of their lives.

However, the females only live alone until they are about three years old.

That is when they are ready to start their own families.

Then they will have cubs of their own to show how to survive in the world.

fully grown
jaguar

Glossary

capybaras
(ka-pee-BAR-uhs)
large rodents
that live in South
America

cubs (KUHBZ)
the babies of an animal
such as a jaguar

dens (DENZ)
homes where
animals can rest,
hide from enemies,
and have babies

pounce
(POUNSS)
to jump suddenly
to catch an
animal

prey (PRAY)
animals that are eaten
by other animals

rain forest (RAYN for-ist)
a large, warm area of
land covered with trees
and plants, where lots
of rain falls

23

Index

Read more

Ganeri, Anita. *Jaguar (A Day in the Life: Rain Forest Animals)*. Chicago: Heinemann-Raintree (2011).

Guidone, Julie. *Jaguars (Animals that Live in the Rainforest)*. New York: Weekly Reader Early Learning Library (2009).

Huntrods, David. *Jaguars (Amazing Animals)*. New York: Weigl Publishers (2007).

Learn more online

To learn more about jaguars, visit
www.bearportpublishing.com/JungleBabies

About the author

Rachel Lynette has written more than 100 nonfiction books for children. She also creates resources for teachers. Rachel lives near Seattle, Washington. She enjoys biking, hiking, crocheting hats, and spending time with her family and friends.